Timo
and the soft white light

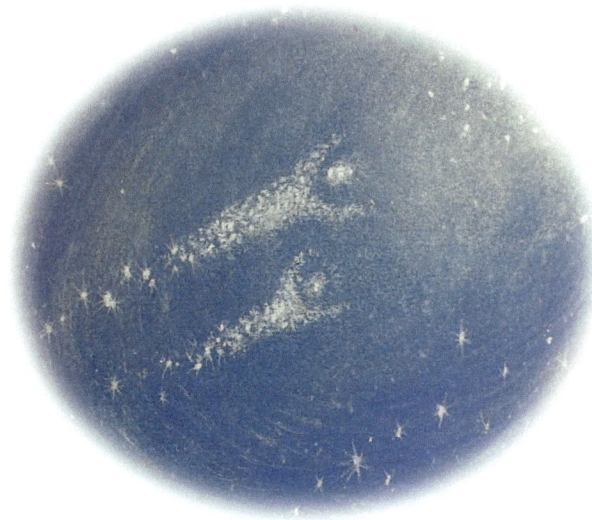

Margreet Meijer
Kaly Cotteleer

Written by:
Margreet Meijer
chaplain
The Netherlands

Illustrated by:
Kaly Cotteleer
artistic therapeutist
Belgium

Translated from Dutch by:
Liesbeth Meyer
author
The Netherlands

Published by:
Graviant educational publications, Doetinchem, The Netherlands

ISBN: 9789492593290

Thus the Prophet spoke:
You wish to know the secret of death,
but how will you find it,
unless you search in the heart of life?

From: "The Prophet" by Kahlil Giban

Autumn has come.

Timo and Grandpa are in the woods.

Grandpa is looking after Timo today.

'Hold on tight, Timo', Grandpa says.

'We'll send the kite off together.

The wind will take it high into the sky.'

Fluffy is there as well.

He pulls on the string.

Well done Fluffy,

the kite goes up to the clouds.

Timo and Grandpa are tired from flying the kite.

They're home again.

Grandpa's big chair is next to the window.

A blackbird is looking in the window.

He sees Timo and Grandpa and all of Timo's pets.

'Come and sit next to me', Grandpa says.

He reads Timo a nice story.

Gently Timo strokes Grandpa's comfy sweater

and tickles his beard under his chin.

It is such a lovely day.

Grandpa is taken ill.
The doctor tells him
he has to go to the hospital.
Timo, Mum and Dad go there as well,
to visit Grandpa.
Fluffy sits on Timo's shoulder,
next to his ear.
He whispers: 'I'm scared of this place.'
'No, don't be afraid', Timo says,
'we're close together, aren't we?'

In the hospital Grandpa is lying in a very large bed.

He's not wearing his comfy sweater today.

There's a blanket covering him instead.

He speaks quite softly, almost as softly as Fluffy.

'Hello dears', he says. 'How nice to see you all.'

Timo looks at Grandpa lying in the big bed.

Fluffy looks under the bed.

'I've got a plan', Fluffy says. 'Come along.'

Timo and Fluffy crawl under the bed.

Is the bed a castle? Is Grandpa the King?

Timo and Fluffy pretend to be the knights guarding the castle.

Watch out, we have to take good care of the King!

Hold up your sword and chase away all danger!

Dad holds Timo and takes him to Grandpa.

'My darling Timo', Grandpa whispers.

'I'm so ill. I am old and I think I will die soon.'

Timo keeps very quiet.

He looks at Grandpa's face, his glasses and his dear eyes.

He digs in his pocket. There he finds his most precious chestnut from the woods.

'This one is for you Grandpa!'

Timo gives Grandpa his biggest hug.

Grandpa smiles, saying: 'You will always be my darling grandson forever!'

Grandpa is very ill and so tired.

He closes his eyes again.

Goodbye Grandpa, have a nice sleep.

Just stay in bed in the hospital.

The doctor and nurse will look after you.

Later on Timo falls asleep, in his own bed.

Timo is asleep in his own cosy bed.

He is dreaming.

Together with Grandpa

he is flying in the sky.

Up they go,

even higher than the clouds.

And Fluffy comes too.

Timo wakes up.

Mum and dad are feeling sad.

'What's wrong?' Timo asks.

'Come and sit with us',

mum and dad say.

'Grandpa died during the night.

An angel took him away

to the soft white light.'

Where is Timo today?

Timo is scared.

He's hiding quietly

behind the curtains.

Can you see his little toes?

Come out Timo,

I've found you.

There is Timo, thank goodness!

He wants to visit Grandpa.
He goes out on his red bike.
Fluffy is sitting in the back.
Are you all right, Fluffy?
Hold on, we are going on a journey.

Timo is very good at cycling his bike.
He pedals so fast and the wheels turn round.
He pedals out of the garden, onto the pavement and past all the houses,
all the way to the end of the street,
there are the woods.

Timo rushes as fast as he can.
Where are you both going, Timo and Fluffy?

'Timo, where are you?'

That's mum. She's found Timo.

'I have some chestnuts', he says.

'These are for Grandpa, in the Land of Light.'

'Timo, my darling', Mum says.

'Come with me.'

Mum gives Timo a big hug.

He likes being close to her.

Timo snuggles close to his mum.

'I want to see Grandpa.'

Mum gently strokes Timo's hair.

'That's not possible, Timo,

Grandpa's life here has ended.

He had grown old and sick.

It is not possible for him to be with us anymore.

But the light is still here for each of us.

It will be here to help you to grow into a big, strong boy.'

'We'll find Grandpa a nice place,
where he will be buried.'

Timo and Mum take the chestnuts
to where Grandpa is buried.
Close to Grandpa's grave Timo digs a big hole in the ground.
He puts all the chestnuts into the hole.
They will grow into a huge tree one day.

Wintertime has come.

It is quiet everywhere.

The blackbird is sitting in a tree.

Listen, he is singing.

He is singing his songs

about the soft white light

and about Timo's dear Grandpa.

And about Timo becoming

a big strong boy.

Springtime has come!
Everything flowers and grows.
Timo has also grown.
He doesn't look for Grandpa anymore.
He looks around. He feels Grandpa everywhere:
in the chestnut tree, in the butterfly, in the breeze.

But most of all he feels Grandpa inside himself,
whenever he thinks of Grandpa's dear eyes.
When he remembers kite-flying with Grandpa,
or when he thinks of all the nice stories while sitting in the big chair.

When he thinks of Grandpa he feels so close to him.
As close as can be.
Just like the soft white light.

Loss and bereavement

When children face death, as an adult we often stand empty handed. It affects our insecurities, our own questions about life and death and our religious upbringing, whether in the past or now in the present.

In 'Timo and the soft white light' is spoken from the young child's perspective. The book does not offer a fitting answer nor facts about the process of dying. Timo's story is light-hearted and leaves plenty of room to communicate and find words together from the child's level within one's own life's theological background in search for the 'secret of life.'

Children handle loss of a loved one in different ways and are unable to cope with the loss and saying farewell. In some cases we could be surprised how fast a young child is able to move on, however the child can be disconsolate as well. When adults show it's all right to have sorrow and questions are allowed, the child will feel safe and secure.

To Timo there is comfort in the closeness of his parents and his bond with nature. He experiences a profound vitality that reaches beyond death. This helps him to move on, to play and become 'a big strong boy.'